A Very Nice Lunch

by Celeste Albright
illustrated by Cheryl Mendenhall

 HOUGHTON MIFFLIN   BOSTON

Printed in China

ISBN-13: 978-0-547-01751-8
ISBN-10: 0-547-01751-0

15 16 17 18 0940 20 19 18 17
4500634148

"I have a banana
in my lunch box.
I don't like bananas,"
said Horse.

"I will take it,"
said Monkey.
"I like bananas."

"I have a bone
in my lunch box,"
said Rabbit.
"I don't like bones!"

"I will take that bone,"
said Dog.
"I like bones."

"My lunch box
has an apple in it,"
said Dog.
"I don't like apples."

"I will take the apple,"
said Horse.
"I like apples a lot!"

"I have a fish
in my lunch bag,"
said Cat.
"I **love** fish!"

Rabbit and Dog and Horse
and Monkey looked at
the lunch boxes.
They were all mixed up!

They changed lunch boxes.
And they all had
a very nice lunch.

Responding

Understanding Characters A cat and a dog are characters in this story. What do they say and do? What does this tell you about them? Make a chart.

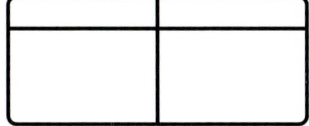

Write About It

Text to World Draw three pictures of a boy or girl eating lunch. Label the pictures "First," "Next," and "Last."

WORDS TO KNOW

do	look
down	off
have	out
help	take

LEARN MORE WORDS

banana	boxes

TARGET SKILL **Understanding Characters** Tell more about characters.

TARGET STRATEGY **Summarize** Stop to tell important events as you read.

GENRE **Fiction** is a story that is made up.